MINDFUL ME
Breath by Breath

Every emotion is an adventure …

First published in Great Britain in 2018 by
The Watts Publishing Group

ISBN: 978 1 4451 5703 0 (hbk)
ISBN: 978 1 4451 5704 7 (pbk)

Managing editor: Victoria Brooker
Creative design: Lisa Peacock

Printed in China

FSC
www.fsc.org
MIX
Paper from
responsible sources
FSC® C104740

Franklin Watts is a division of
Hachette Children's Books,
an Hachette UK company.
Carmelite House
50 Victoria Embankment
London EC4Y 0DZ

www.hachette.co.uk
www.franklinwatts.co.uk

MINDFUL ME
Breath by Breath

A Mindfulness Guide to Feeling Calm

Written by
Paul Christelis

W
FRANKLIN
WATTS

Illustrated by
Elisa Paganelli

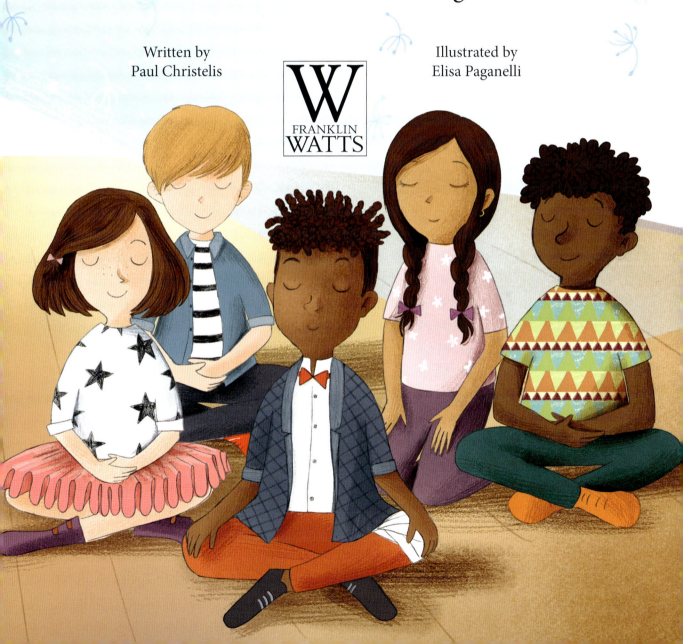

HOW TO USE THIS BOOK

Mindfulness is a way of paying attention to our present moment experience with an attitude of kindness and curiosity. Most of the time, our attention is distracted – often by thoughts about the past or future – and this can make us feel jumpy, worried, self-critical and confused.

By gently moving our focus from our busy minds and into the present moment, we begin to let go of distraction and learn to tap into the ever-present supply of joy and ease that resides in the here-and-now. Mindfulness can also help us to improve concentration, calm unpleasant emotions, even boost our immune systems.

In this book, children are encouraged to develop mindfulness by using their breathing as an 'object' to pay attention to. Breathing happens naturally, in the present moment, and simply noticing the sensations of the breath can instil a sense of peace and calm.

Readers are also invited to gratefully acknowledge the gift of life bestowed by each breath. Cultivating this attitude of gratitude helps us to experience life as wondrous and special, even in times of difficulty.

The book can be read interactively, allowing readers to pause at various points and bring their attention to what they are noticing. The ▸PAUSE BUTTON in the text suggests where you might encourage readers to be curious about what they observe, for example the texture or temperature of the breath. Each time this ▸PAUSE BUTTON is used, mindfulness is deepened.

Don't rush this pause; really allow enough time for children to stay with their experience. It doesn't matter if what they feel or notice is pleasant or unpleasant: what's important is to pay attention to it with a friendly attitude. This will introduce them to a way of being in the world that promotes calmness, health and happiness.

This is the story of three very different children who have one very important thing in common. In fact, they also have something in common with you! Yes, the you who is reading this book right now.

Do you have any idea what Sam, Lenny, Selina and you all share? Here's a clue: it can't be seen, and unless you are running or exercising it probably can't be heard. But if you are very still, close your eyes, and concentrate on what's happening in your body, you will feel it.

Try it now! Close your eyes and see if you can notice what's happening in your body. Can you feel something moving?

▸ PAUSE BUTTON

Aha! What we all share is BREATH! Without it, we wouldn't be alive, so it's very important indeed. But we hardly notice that we are breathing, unless we are out of breath, or feeling ill.

For Sam, it doesn't matter if he is feeling well or sick, everyday he spends a few minutes noticing his breathing. He does this each morning, sitting up in bed. Noticing his breathing helps him feel calm and relaxed. A great way to start the day!

You might wonder, 'How can I notice MY breathing?' It's easy! All you need to do is sit up straight, let your body relax, and close your eyes. Imagine that you are a cat sitting perfectly still, or maybe a tree – upright and strong.

Now, see if you can feel the air moving into your nose as you breath in, and feel the air moving out of your nose as you breath out. Just let breathing happen as it usually does, without trying to breath in a special way.

Take a minute to feel your breath moving in and out of your nose. You can also feel the breath moving in your belly. Try placing your hand on your belly and feel it moving up and down as you breathe for another minute.

 PAUSE BUTTON

Maybe, like Sam, you noticed that your mind can be quite busy while you're focusing attention on your breath. You can get lost in thoughts, memories, or **worries**.

If that happens, try silently counting your breaths. Every in-breath and out-breath is counted as one full breath. See if you can take ten full breaths. Counting in this way helps your mind to be less distracted.

Sam is now on his way to school. He doesn't know it yet, but today he will help two other children to feel better by simply **noticing** their breathing.

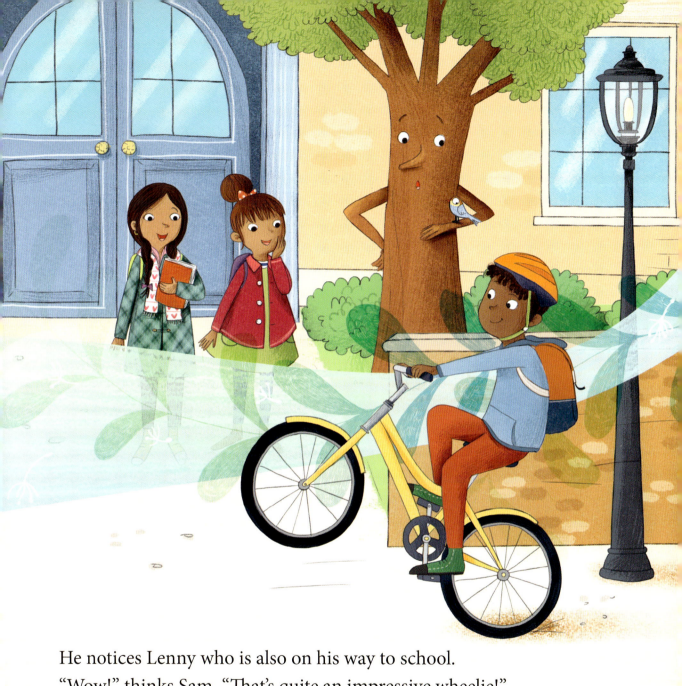

He notices Lenny who is also on his way to school.
"Wow!" thinks Sam. "That's quite an impressive wheelie!"

Lenny is a little too confident and loses concentration. Before he knows it, he loses balance and, well, you can see what happens!

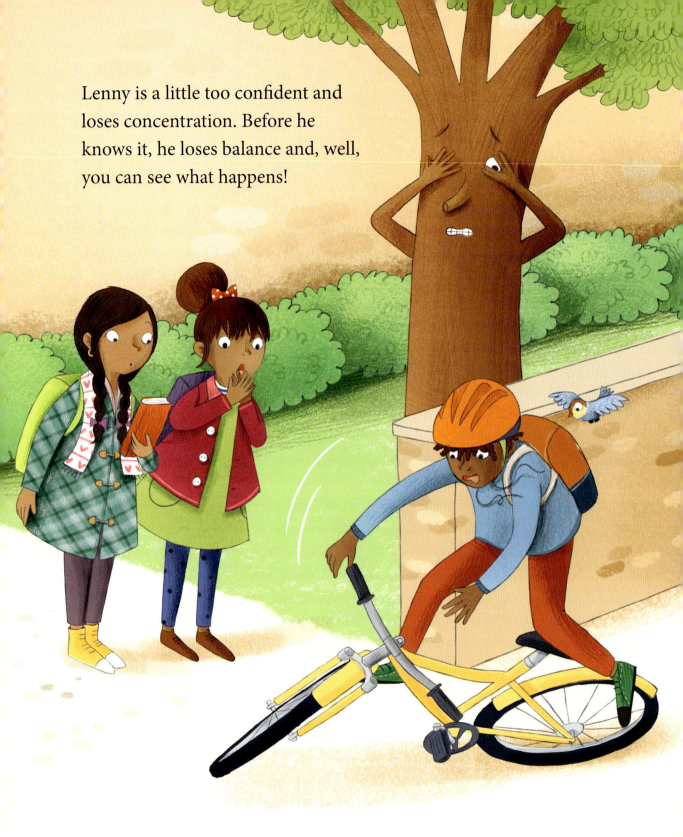

Sam runs over to help Lenny whose knee is badly scraped.
Lenny sees the blood, feels the stinging and starts to panic.
"What if I have to go to the hospital?"

Luckily, Sam has some good advice to help Lenny calm down.

"It's best not to worry about what might happen later. What really helps is to pay attention to your breathing. This will **relax** you, and when you relax you don't feel the pain as much."

Sam was right! After a minute or two of noticing his breathing, Lenny still feels the pain in his knee, but it's not as bad.

When was the last time you felt something painful? See if you can picture yourself in that situation. Now, see yourself breathing slow and deep breaths even while the pain is there. You can imagine your breaths are friendly and smiley, just like Sam!

Later that day, after school, Sam is attending concert rehearsal. He's playing guitar. Tonight the whole school will watch him.

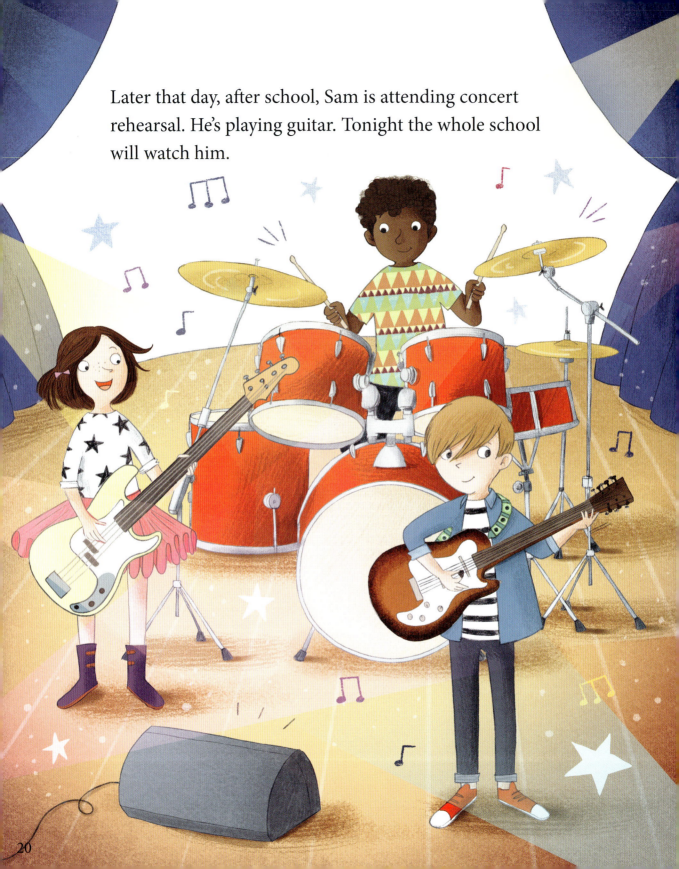

This is Selina. She's singing in the show. It's her first time on stage so she's already **nervous**! It's so hard to rehearse when her head is filled with worries.

This looks like a job for … Super Sam! "I'm nervous too," he tells Selina while they take a break. "Let me show you how to feel more **confident**."

Sam shows Selina how to concentrate on her breathing, just as he did with Lenny. She counts ten full breaths and begins to feel calmer.

"And now," says Sam, "see if you can notice how each breath feels. Is it rough? Smooth? Shallow or deep? Cool or warm?"

"Hmm," wonders Selina.
"I've never noticed! Let me see …"

Have you ever noticed how your breath feels? Take a moment now, close your eyes, and be curious. See if you can use three different words to describe what you notice.

 PAUSE BUTTON

There is no such thing as a right or a wrong breath. Every breath is different. You can never breathe the same breath twice!

It's later that evening, and Selina is waiting to go on stage. There are so many people in the audience! Her tummy feels full of butterflies, but she is not worried.

The concert is a **success**! Sam and the band play well, Selina hits her high notes, and the audience give a standing ovation …

"Bravo!" says the head teacher, congratulating the children after the show. "Well done, everyone. What a breath of fresh air that was!"

She doesn't realise how right she is! A breath of fresh air is always there to help us when we need it!

NOTES FOR PARENTS AND TEACHERS

Here are a few other mindfulness exercises and breathing suggestions to add to your child's Mindful Toolkit. These are simple, effective and, above all, fun to do!

BALLOON IN THE BELLY

Breathing deeply into the belly (diaphragmatic breathing) supports a calm and relaxed body and mind. This practice helps children to shift their breathing from the chest into the belly (and is equally beneficial for adults too!).

To really feel the effects of this, lie down on a bed or the floor, close your eyes and begin to notice your breathing. After a few breaths, place one hand on your chest and feel how far your hand moves as you breathe. Then, place your hand on your belly, and notice the amount of movement there. If there is more movement in the chest than in the belly, then that tells you that you're not breathing deeply enough with the diaphragm.

You can encourage your child to breathe more deeply by inviting her to imagine that there is a balloon in her belly that inflates when she breathes in, and deflates on the out-breath. Ask her to choose the colour of the balloon, and then with eyes closed to imagine it filling with the breath, and emptying. She can keep her hands on her belly as she does this. If she becomes distracted by sounds or thoughts, then she can notice the distraction and choose to return her attention to her balloon.

A variation on this practice might be to do it in the bath, where your child can watch the belly rising out of the water. Placing a bath toy on the belly can also be fun: try to breathe smoothly and evenly so that the toy doesn't fall off into the water.

7 - 11 BREATHING

This practice is particularly helpful if you or your child is feeling overwhelmed or anxious, or simply if you want to relax.

Breathe in through the nose to the count of seven, pause, and then breathe out through the nose to the count of eleven. This ensures that the out-breath is longer than the in-breath, which enables the parasympathetic nervous system (PSN) to kick in. The PSN is responsible for calming the stress response in the body so activating it when stressed is an effective way to regulate physiological and emotional arousal.

You can also experiment with using shorter countdowns, for example, breathing in to the count of five and out to the count of nine. Be careful not to rush the counting, though. Allow each breath enough space and time to reach its full length.

BREATHE IN THE GOOD

In this exercise, children are encouraged to focus their attention on nourishing and affirming aspects of their lives.

First, ask them to call to mind something that makes them feel good, happy, or safe. Examples might be: a relationship with a close friend, family member or pet; a place in which they feel content and safe, such as a bedroom, a special tree in the garden, the seaside; or something they feel grateful for – the kindness of a grandparent, meals cooked by mum or dad, the opportunity to learn how to play a musical instrument. Then, as they inhale, they imagine breathing in all the good feelings associated with this particular person, place or object. Exhaling, they imagine breathing out these feelings and sharing them with the world so that everyone might benefit from this nourishing, positive energy.

Repeat this sequence a few times and then notice how it feels to take in and give out such happy vibes!

FURTHER READING

Acorns to Great Acorns: Meditations for Children, Marie Delanote
   (Findhorn Press Ltd, 2017)

Glad to be Dan: Discover How Mindfulness Helps Dan to Be Happy Every Day,
   Jo Howarth and Jude Lennon (CreateSpace Independent Publishing Platform, 2016)

Master of Mindfulness: How to be Your Own Superhero in Times of Stress, Laurie Grossman
   (New Harbinger, 2016)

Mindful Monkey, Happy Panda, Lauren Alderfer and Kerry Lee McLean
   (Wisdom Publications, 2011)

Mindful Movements: Ten Exercises for Well-being, Wietske Vriezen
   (Parallax Press, 2008)

Planting Seeds: Practicing Mindfulness with Children, Thich Nhat Hanh
   (Parallax Press, 2011)

Sitting Still Like a Frog, Eline Snel
   (Shambhala Publications Inc., 2014)